Steam around
NORTH NORFOLK

C. G. Beckett

BECKNELL BOOKS

NORWICH AND KING'S LYNN

First published 1981

© Becknell Books 1981

ISBN 0 907087 03 5

BECKNELL BOOKS
P.O. BOX 21
KING'S LYNN
PE30 2QP

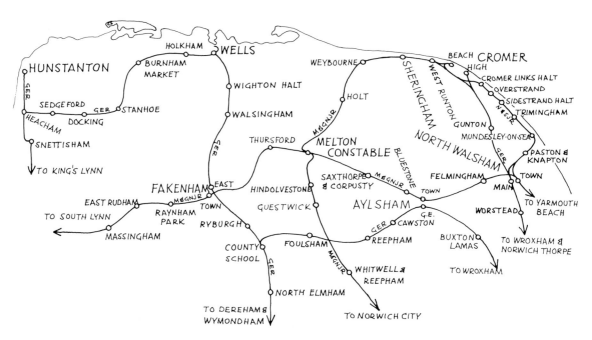

MAP OF THE RAILWAY LINES AROUND NORTH NORFOLK

Designed by Becknell Studio

Printed in Great Britain by Witley Press Ltd., Hunstanton

Introduction

Steam railways first entered North Norfolk with the extension of the Dereham-Fakenham branch to Wells in December 1857, largely through the efforts of the Earl of Leicester. In the north-west corner of Norfolk, the *Lynn & Hunstanton* Directors replaced horse buses with trains in 1862 and built lodging houses, realising the popularity of this coastal stretch following the Prince of Wales' purchase of Sandringham House. The Heacham-Wells *West Norfolk Junction Railway* opened in 1866 but had little effect on the agricultural area it served.

Not till 1877, when on 26th March Cromer High opened, did railways extend to the north-east part. Little tourist potential was seen and only the extension of the *Eastern & Midlands Railway* to Cromer Beach in 1887 (from Melton Constable) spurred the GER to provide the direct Liverpool Street *Cromer Express,* incidentally popularising Cromer Crabs in London! The Midland and the Great Northern railways, taking over the E&MR in 1893 as the M&GN, saw the potential of serving prosperous Midlands holidaymakers. The M&GN extended in 1898 from North Walsham to Mundesley, and, encouraged by royal visits to *Poppyland* in 1897, joined forces in the form of the *Norfolk & Suffolk Joint* to avoid further duplication with the GER. The Overstrand route opened in 1906, with link lines between the two companies at Cromer. The structure of North Norfolk's railways, based on holiday traffic and agricultural freight, was then complete.

Wartime activities along the invasion coast broke the tourist and farming routine. The LNER had absorbed the GER in 1923 and the M&GN in 1936. Melton stopped repairing locos in 1937 although remained an important depot. Nationalisation meant little change but the 1950s saw a struggle for survival.

The 1953 floods so damaged the Heacham-Wells line that only parts were ever re-opened but the popularity of Walsingham shrine kept open the Dereham-Wells line until 1964, even after the silting up of Wells harbour. *Poppyland* holiday traffic declined and closure of the army camps led to changes there. Conductor-guards and through services were tried on the N&S line and fortunes briefly revived with the closure of Cromer High; platform lengthening and a new turntable (in 1954) enabled Beach to take *Broadsman* and *Norfolkman* expresses, hauled by some of the largest locos ever to enter North Norfolk. However, falling demand led to North Walsham-Mundesley push-and-pull services in 1953 (the line onto Cromer having closed that year) followed by dmus in 1956. A similar fate was suffered by the Melton-Sheringham line in 1957; named trains were withdrawn in June 1962. On 12th September 1960 the Themelthorpe loop (for freight off the Norwich City-Melton line direct to Wroxham) was opened, heralding final closure of the Melton-Sheringham line in 1964, five years after the closure of the rest of the M&GN.

The Duke of Edinburgh rode the last steam train on 30th May 1963, the royal special going to Weybourne for stabling. The Hunstanton-King's Lynn line operated with dmus until 1969. The rest of the depleted diesel network just survives today.

In preparing this book, the following have rendered great assistance: E. Blakey, GGS Photography, Norwich, C.I.M. Shewring, A. C. Whittaker and the staff of Witley Press Sales Ltd., Hunstanton. To all of these, my thanks. The photographers are as follows: Dr. Ian C. Allen — 9, 16, 17, 19, 21, 27, 36; H. C. Casserley — 7; late T. G. Hepburn, courtesy Mrs. Hepburn — 4, 6, 42, 43, 44, 46; H. N. James — 37, 47; Lens of Sutton — 2, 45; L&GRP collection, courtesy David & Charles — 35; Dr. W. J. Naunton — 8, 12, 25, 31, 32, 33, 49, 50; L. R. Peters — 18, 22, 34, 38, 39, Front cover; Real Photographs Co. Ltd — 13, 40; N. E. Stead — 26; late E. Tuddenham, courtesy M&GN Circle — 10, 11, 14, 15, 20, 23, 24, 28, 29, 30; P. Waylett — 1; G. A. Yeomans — 3, 5, 41, 48. I am very pleased to acknowledge their superb contributions.

C. G. Beckett
January 1981

Front cover : D16/3 62523, Runton West Junction, 17th June 1952.

Steam around North Norfolk

1. North Norfolk covers the coastal area from Heacham to Mundesley. Entering Heacham, ex-GE D16/3 4-4-0 62606 hauls a Hunstanton-Liverpool Street express.

2. The GE Hunstanton terminus was extended in 1899 with the building of the company's own hotel. *Intermediate* 2-4-0 479 blows off whilst the driver awaits his holidaymaker load.

3. July 1953 and *Claud Hamilton* D16/3 4-4-0 62534 eases out of Hunstanton past the turntable, carrying another load of holidaymakers on the 10.13 a.m. to King's Lynn.

4. Another *Intermediate* — 62797 — leaves Hunstanton tender-first with a Wells local. The train of elderly stock, including a noteworthy gas wagon, would be reversed at Heacham for the branch.

5. Wells saw disappointingly little holiday traffic, remaining a peaceful country terminus. *Claud Hamilton* 4-4-0 62564 of Norwich Thorpe simmers gently outside the locoshed.

6. D16/3 62545, outstationed at Wells, leaves with a Sunday train for Norwich Thorpe. This photograph demonstrates clearly the style of lettering prevalent in the early 1950s.

7. A similar viewpoint, but Wells on 29th June 1936 saw *Humpty Dumpty* D13 4-4-0 8030 at the platform. The functional shed and antiquated shunt signal are of especial interest.

8. The branch loco facilities were well-maintained, even after the onset of dieselisation. In August 1956, D16/3 4-4-0 62522 approaches the coaling wagon in front of Wells turntable.

9. Cutting across the GE lines was the cross-country M&GN system. During 1936 the LMS loaned the *Joint* Johnson 3P 4-4-0 759, seen on a mixed rake near Massingham.

10. One of the ubiquitous Ivatt 4MT 2-6-0s — 43110 — takes the curve at East Rudham with a cattle special from Fakenham M&GN on 21st May 1958. Cattle wagons pre-date the movement of livestock by road.

11. On 2nd August 1958 Nottingham-based 4F 0-6-0 43954, heading the 8.19 a.m. Yarmouth Beach to Chesterfield, is about to collect the token automatically at Raynham Park.

12. County School was the junction of the GE Wells to Wymondham line and the East Norfolk branch to Wroxham. Unfitted Holden J17 0-6-0 65573 heads an up pick-up freight.

13. Another J17 0-6-0, 65567, on a RCTS special in March 1962. By then Foulsham was the terminus of the truncated East Norfolk branch from County School.

14. N7/1 0-6-2T 69709 is seen on 26th July 1951 between Reepham and Foulsham with the 2.33 p.m. Wroxham to Dereham passenger, formed of a mixture of GE and LNER stock.

15. Whitwell & Reepham saw 4MT 43111 shunt its ballast train to let D16/3 62515 pass with the 9.37 a.m. Melton Constable to Norwich City passenger on 6th September 1957.

16. A classic LNER scene of D16/3 62561 with five Gresley bogies, yet the M&GN milepost indicates the location as Hindolvestone. The train is a Melton to Norwich City local.

17. Johnson 4-4-0s 75 and 39 draw 15 six-wheelers out of Melton Constable in 1928. Melton, the heart of the M&GN system, linked three branches with the Midlands route.

18. Melton Works closed for loco repairs in 1936, but remained an important depot. LMS Ivatt 4MT 2-6-0s, introduced after nationalisation, are evident in this shot of 15th June 1952.

19. 4MT 43147 brings the Cromer portion of the *Leicester,* the Yarmouth Beach to Birmingham express, across Melton West Junction. Two headlamps signify this two-coach train as an express!

20. Gresley J39 0-6-0 64803 stands at Melton's island platform in May 1953 about to depart tender-first with the breakdown train, complete with inspectors saloon and clerestoried riding van.

21. Although Holden J67/2 0-6-0T 68536 — built Stratford, April 1892 — was officially classified 2F, it still found itself on the Melton down crossover with a class 1 passenger duty.

22. On 17th June 1951 Melton Constable shed sheltered D16/3 4-4-0s 62515 and 62610. The *Claud Hamiltons* were not ideal on the *Leicesters* and were eventually replaced by six-coupled B12s.

23. Vacuum-fitted Holden J17 0-6-0 65581 passes Melton Constable East box in this panoramic view. The sc
loco more GE. Built Stratford 1910, this carries a Whitaker automatic tablet catcher for M&GN use. Whit

es a good idea of the mixture to be found in North Norfolk: the location could not be more M&GN nor the
roduced this on the S&DJR, the M&GN adopting it in 1906 following injury to a fireman.

24. Doncaster *standard* 4MT 2-6-0 76034 makes a contrast to the usual Ivatt 4MT *moguls.* Working furiously, it heads a northbound freight tender-first through Melton Constable.

25. Sadly, this picture of the 12.56 p.m. Yarmouth Beach to Peterborough North is dated 28th February 1959: closure day. Embellished 4MT 2-6-0 43145 loads at Corpusty & Saxthorpe.

26. Another 4MT — 43107 — brings an afternoon Yarmouth-bound passenger into Aylsham North, watched by schoolboys. The tall signal box and up starter repeater indicate the sharp approach bend.

27. The Cromer branch singled at Brinningham Single Line Junction, just over a mile out of Melton. D16/3 62597 heads towards Cromer past the delightful GN-style somersaults.

28. B12/3 4-6-0 61568 brings the 9.39 a.m. Melton-Cromer Beach down Kelling Bank on 19th June 1957. Trains passed in the level section at Weybourne, roughly half-way down the gradient.

29. Climbing tender-first out of Weybourne, Ivatt 4MT 2-6-0 43147 hauls the 9.40 a.m. Cromer Beach to Birmingham New Street, formed of ex LMS stock, towards Kelling cutting on 19th June 1957.

30. 43153 rolls down to Weybourne with the Cromer portion of the 9.31 a.m. ex Norwich City on the same day. The distant indicates a stop at Weybourne — to pass an up express.

31. *Claud Hamilton* D16/3 62515 climbs out of Weybourne towards Kelling in August 1955. The gradients either side of Weybourne are 1 in 80, giving the locos some work to do!

32. In the same month, Ivatt 4MT 2-6-0 43108 coasts to the foot of the gradient with a three-coach Cromer to Melton stopping train, ready to tackle the bank up to Weybourne.

33. August 1955 saw beautifully turned-out D16/3 62578 of Norwich Thorpe shed bringing an inspection saloon into Sheringham. The class 1 headcode is shown by the GER disc.

34. The *Broadsman* was *pacific* powered to Sheringham. Proving the point, A5 4-6-2T 69835 hauls the two-coach Sheringham portion on to West Runton on 21st June 1951.

35. GE Bromley E10 0-4-4T 058 at Runton West Junction in 1908. The red-and-white disc indicates single-line working from the Norfolk & Suffolk Overstrand line.

36. Taking the same route on a rainy day some fifty years later, B12/3 61540 also takes the tablet. The contrast between photographs lies mainly in the stock and motive power.

37. Going the opposite way in August 1961, Thompson B1 4-6-0 61043 crosses tender-first over to the GE to start the 1 in 80 climb towards Newstead Lane Junction.

38. Although in M&GN territory, this scene is dominated by Worsdell F4 2-4-2T 67162 and Great Eastern coaches accelerating out of Cromer Beach on 19th June 1951.

39. Cromer Beach is a lovely terminus, looking rural or urban depending on view. The country branch is illustrated by sister F6 2-4-2Ts 67225 and 67224 on shed in June 1951.

40. Redevelopment of Cromer Beach leads to this scene in September 1954, with B12/3 4-6-0 61540 at the front of an unidentified *Sandringham* B17 4-6-0 in the shadows.

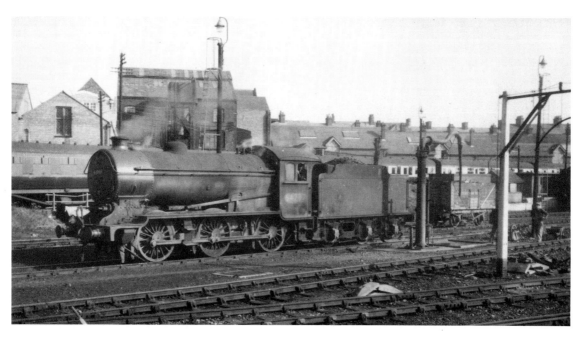

41. The faster pace of the late 1950s saw J39 0-6-0 64797 in September 1957 on a rather more industrial-looking Cromer Beach yard. Gresley introduced this 4P5F class in 1926.

42. The *Eastern Belle* Pullman ran to different resorts daily between 1929 and 1939. B17 4-6-0 2827 *Aske Hall* pulls along the GE section from Cromer Beach on to Norwich.

43. LNER *Intermediate* E4 2-4-0 7416 brings a slow passenger into Cromer High past the Junction box. The connection down the hill is the GE access line to the M&GN at East Runton.

44. The Up *Norfolkman* leaves Cromer High behind D16/3 62584, bound for Liverpool Street. The GE-pattern disc shows it running as an ordinary passenger as far as Norwich.

45. Cromer High in GE days shows a *Claud Hamilton* in its original condition; the shiny smokebox ring and slotted valences are especially noteworthy, as are the lower quadrants.

46. Thompson L1 2-6-4T 67798 leaves Gunton with the down *Broadsman*. This was another Liverpool Street express which became a stopping passenger on the Norwich to Sheringham section.

47. The typical M&GN somersault gives a clear road to 4MT 2-6-0 43159 seen leaving North Walsham Town for Melton Constable in 1953. The branch arm was for the Mundesley line.

48. Adjacent to the Town station was the GE's Main — still open but now unstaffed. Thompson L1 2-6-4T 67707 pulls in with the 5.47 p.m. to Melton Constable on 7th September 1957.

49. Mundesley was originally built as an elegant M&GN terminus before the through route to Overstrand was opened. N7 0-6-2T 69698 is bound for North Walsham in BR days.

50. Typically GE is Worsdell J15 0-6-0 65469 on a Norfolk Railway Society *engine driving special* at Mundesley on 15th May 1960. Also seen is one of the famous camping coaches.